A Tree Is a Community

BY **David L. Harrison**

ILLUSTRATED BY **Kate Cosgrove**

books for a better earth

™

holiday house • new york

A **Books for a Better Earth**™ Title
The Books for a Better Earth™ collection is designed to inspire
young people to become active, knowledgeable participants in
caring for the planet they live on.
Focusing on solutions to climate change challenges and human
environmental impacts, the collection looks at how
scientists, activists, and young leaders are working
to safeguard Earth's future.

To the poets in my 2011 poetry workshop, now good friends and colleagues:
Joy Frelinger, Cory Corrado, Jeanne Poland, Susan Carmichael,
Rebecca Menshen, Ken Slesarik, Heidi Mordhorst, and Carol-Ann Hoyte.
With affection –D.H.

For Bridget –K.C.

Special thanks to Christine Rollinson, PhD, Forest Ecologist, The Morton Arboretum,
and Bob and Barb Kipfer, Missouri Master Naturalists, for their expert review of the text.

Library of Congress Cataloging-in-Publication Data is available.

ISBN: 978-0-8234-5558-4 (hardcover)

In spring,
the rain
ROARS!
GUSHES!
POURS
down through that
rich,
dark
soil.

The air and ground
warm up, and
the rain
SHOUTS,
"Wake up,
you lazy roots!"

And the roots
wake up
and say,

"Oh yes!
Give us a nice,
long drink
of your good water!"

Next thing you know,
PRESTO–
sap inside
those cold,
bare limbs
gets busy!
Leaves
UNFOLD
like a
new dress.

Buds
DAZZLE
on tips of bony twigs
like fancy
store-bought rings.

Those buds
POP
open,
and bees
BUZZ,
and rain
SPLUSHES,

and sun
SIZZLES,
and before long
seeds grow and—
WHOOSH—
those seeds
let go and reach
the ground,
eager to get started
in that rich, dark soil.

And bugs say,
"Look! A nice tree!"
and they
CRAWL and
CLIMB and
SCURRY up that trunk.

And robins
look like
they've FLOWN
to the twig store
and the mud store,
TOTED back supplies
to build
their fancy nests.

Well, don't you know,
the first eggs
CRACK open,
and right away
mamas and papas
are FLITTING
and FLAPPING
to keep their cheepers
happy.
Yes!

And ants?
Oh my!
Those ants
DASH
like they're running
across a
hot skillet!
And lizards
CROUCH
and wait
till something
tasty
mistakes by too close.

16

Now squirrels
LEAP
and ACROBAT around,
and spiders
HANG webs
like sticky curtains
so moths not looking
get WRAPPED up
in their work.

And the tree
is BUSY
with tree business.
When storms HOWL
and thunder goes
BOOM! BOOM! BOOM!
she HOLDS her families
safe in her STRONG arms.

The tree
GROWS and
STRETCHES,
and new birds
PECK and
DRILL
holes,
and new owls
and opossums
and raccoons
SETTLE in.
And maybe
they make
their own babies?
For sure!

Pretty soon,
summer comes.
HOT! HOT!
Turns OFF the rain.
Grass looks DONE
like just from the OVEN.

Then fall dials
BACK the heat!
LEAVES brown down
and are KISSED
by the wind
till the tree is BALD
as a grandfather.

24

Winter FREEZES in
like icicles
down your back.
The tree
holds up her BARE arms
and SURRENDERS.

But not for long, my dears.
Spring comes
GREENING back,
and frogs no bigger
than a hiccup
PEEK-A-BOO
from bright new leaves.
They CARRY ON
and SHOW OFF
and FILL UP the night
with their PICK ME songs.

The tree
is BUSY
with tree business.
Her green, green leaves
BREATHE IN the air
that we BREATHE OUT.
Yes!
And those same
green, green leaves
BREATHE OUT the air
that we BREATHE IN!
For sure!

BRANCH

LEAF
- CATCHES DUST
- FILTERS THE AIR
- MAKES OXYGEN

BUD

BLOOM

ROOTS
- SAVES WATER
- HOLDS SOIL

That busy tree
has MORE tree business.
That tree she CATCHES
dust in the air and
SAVES water with
her deep, strong roots.
She HOLDS the soil
from WASHING away
and makes us feel COOLER
when the sun, it LICKS
all over with its
HOT tongue.

31

And best of all,
spring brings
RAIN,
and rain brings
BUDS.
Buds bring
FLOWERS,
and flowers bring
BUZZ.

New seeds
drop
to the
rich,
dark soil.

And before
you know it,
a sprout
SHOOTS up.
And very soon
we will have
a fine new tree.
OH YES!

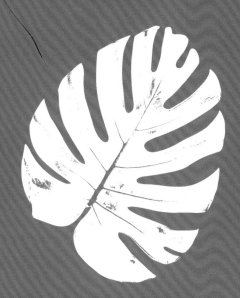

WE AND THE TREE

Trees are among the most important living things on Earth. Some of the reasons are easy to see. Their shade cools us on hot days. Their leaves help keep rain off our heads. They provide shelter and food for all sorts of animals. We cut up dead trees to burn in our fireplace on cold winter nights. We build our houses with lumber from trees.

But trees also help us in ways we cannot see. They remove from the air a chemical known as carbon dioxide, which is the leading cause of global warming. While doing that, trees give off oxygen, another important chemical. We and nearly every other kind of animal on Earth must have oxygen to breathe.

I have a hackberry tree in my backyard. I watch it every day, look for beetles and ants on its bark and birds in its branches. I watch its leaves fall off in Fall and new ones grow in Spring. I call it my tree and I love it. I've taken its picture and written a poem about it. You can have your own tree too, in your yard, in a park, down the street. I think trees love it when we love them.